Earthsongs

Earthsongs

Praying with Nature

Wayne Simsic

Saint Mary's Press
Christian Brothers Publications
Winona, Minnesota

Printed on recycled paper
with soy-based ink

The publishing team for this book included Carl Koch,
FSC, development editor; Rebecca Fairbank, copy editor;
Amy Schlumpf Manion, production editor and typesetter;
Elaine Kohner, illustrator; pre-press, printing, and bind-
ing by the graphics division of Saint Mary's Press.

The acknowledgments continue on page 86.

Printed in the United States of America

Printing: 6 5 4 3 2 1

Year: 1999 98 97 96 95 94 93

ISBN 0-88489-294-8

Somehow it is necessary
to remain close to what is simple;
desire only to nurture the faith
commanded of my heart,
give voice to the creative stirrings within,
find a joyful presence in all things. . . .

To Diana Oberstar,
with love and gratitude

Contents

Introduction

The Need for Nature Prayers

We need prayers—prayers that will heal the open
wounds caused by our misuse of the natural world
and help us to rebuild a healthy relationship with
the earth. Nature prayers can best be expressed
with a childlike heart—a heart that is drawn to
mystery and willing to respond with reverence.
Such prayers bring us barefoot to the earth, sensi-
tive to the moist, rich soil that greets us warmly.
Earth and sky form us, and we open our hands to
the Creator in praise and gratitude.

The need for nature prayers inspired this book,
but that is not its only focus. The book also ad-
dresses the longing each of us has to encounter
nature from the depths of our life. Most of us,
whether or not we feel drawn to participate in a
particular religious tradition, look for spiritual
nourishment in the natural world. We are aware of
a transcendent dimension in nature and seek
paths in the woods, along a shore, in a desert,
or through the heights of a mountain. We find
favorite places that become sacred and reflect our
heart's desire.

Praying with Nature

The natural world reveals God's presence, and that
revelation can move our heart to long more deeply
for God. Revelations of God often come at unexpected times, in a glance of light or in a spring
breeze. The Jesuit poet Gerard Manley Hopkins

talked of how unbelievably deep is the "inscape" in things: a swelling bud, a morning cloud, a white violet.

Nature is turned toward God in praise. When we intimately connect with nature, we can forget our worries for a while and bathe in the mystery of the natural world. Imagine spending an entire day in a favorite landscape, walking through it, appreciating it. Then, as the day draws to a close, you rediscover nature's cycle and develop a new closeness to the earth and sky. Nature's very existence is praise to God; it invites us to sing God's presence too.

Intimate, celebratory experiences of nature offer us a deep respect for its inherent dignity. Love pervades its depths, and amazing mystery awaits close at hand. The psalmists sing:

The heavens proclaim your glory, O God,
and the firmament shows forth
the work of your hands.
Day carries the news to day
and night brings the message to night.
No speech, no word,
no voice is heard;
yet their news goes forth through all the earth,
their words to the farthest bounds of the world.

(Psalm 19:1–4)

Preparation

Preparation can enhance our encounter with natural surroundings. As with any encounter, certain things are asked from us. The following suggestions may be of some help.

First of all, take time to set aside your worries and concerns. If you are outside, concentrate on the nature all around you. If you are meditating indoors, let the scenes suggested by the prayers take hold of your imagination. Greet a landscape with love, realizing that God is at the heart of all physical reality. Focus on the beauty, mystery, and power of nature, and let go of feelings of self-importance. Remember God's words to Job: "'Is it your wisdom that sets the hawk flying . . . ? Does the eagle soar at your command?'" (Job 39:26–27).

Second, relax. Breathe deeply and slowly. Calm your tired body and racing mind. Settle into a deep, peaceful center. Let go of anxiousness, worries, thoughts of unfinished projects, and all other practical concerns. If your mind wanders, gently bring it back to the scene from nature and into communion with God.

Hand over your entire life to God, and ask for the grace to receive nature's revelation. The American philosopher Henry David Thoreau once said that if we go to nature with chaotic hearts, we will soon leave. Thomas Merton wrote that there is no room in the silence of nature for our noisy hearts.

Last of all, rely on the senses. They have their own unique wisdom. Concentrate on experiencing the surroundings through touch, taste, hearing, smell, and sight. Allow your senses immediate contact with nature.

Eventually your body will connect you to the landscape. Nature will enter your mind and imagination in unexpected ways. You may find that as you explore a certain landscape, you begin to know its contours as if they were the contours of your own body. You may realize in new ways that nature forms your consciousness, your very spirituality, and that in opening your senses, you stand open to the Creator.

Ways of Praying in Nature

1. Allow the natural setting you choose to pray in—a beach, a park, a forest, a hill, a garden—to form your prayer. Remain in the landscape for a long period of time, and let the beauty, intricacy, and mystery of the environment inspire you and catapult your heart to God.

2. Contemplate your surroundings. Learn to see from the heart: simply look at and enjoy flowers, trees, water. Spend time before an insignificant object like a rock or a blade of grass and consider how God views the world.

3. Meditate. Nature often opens us to the significant times in our life. For example, watching a stream edge through rocks and along a bank may inspire you to reflect on the changes in your life and the events that formed you.

4. Use God's word, especially the Psalms. The words of the psalmists should be taken to heart and prayed as the heart's expression of the joy and mystery of nature.

5. Recall powerful images from nature during a hectic day to refocus your heart on God.

Using the Prayer Services

Each prayer service in this book has a theme that is meant to give you some direction, though you may find themes of your own rising out of the readings. Follow your heart's lead.

The prayers are short enough to use while walking through the woods or along a shore without breaking up the rhythm of your own response to nature. Most important, take plenty of time to savor each image, each passage, each feeling. Pray slowly, very slowly.

If you use the prayers indoors, take time to imagine yourself in a natural setting, experiencing it as fully as you can. Be patient and give yourself enough time to relax and visualize this setting. Music may help transport your mind to this setting.

You might find that some of the prayer services inspire a response like writing a journal entry, making music, molding clay, painting in watercolor, or responding through some other medium.

As we enter the depths of the natural world and answer God's personal call for us, the world comes alive. This vision changes our heart and transforms our life. Encountering the creative love at the heart of nature, we claim the secret depths of our own soul.

Morning Song

Opening

God, my friend, I celebrate the morning, the beginning of this new day. Let me experience the giftedness of your creation and the grace of my own being as I face the responsibilities that lie before me.

Psalm

My heart is ready, O God;
I will sing, sing your praise
and make music with all my soul.
Awake, lyre and harp.
I will wake the dawn.
I will praise you, Yahweh, among the peoples;
among the nations I will give thanks,
for your love reaches to the heavens
and your faithfulness to the skies.
O God, arise above the heavens;
may your glory be over the earth!

(Psalm 108:1–5)

Reading

The dawn comes slow and cold. Only occasionally, somewhere along the creek or on the slopes above, a bird sings. I have not slept well, and I waken without much interest in the day. I set the camp to rights, and fix breakfast, and eat. The day is clear, and high up on the points and ridges to the west of my camp I can see the sun shining on the woods. And suddenly I am full of an ambition: I want to get up where the sun is; I want to sit still in the sun up there among the high rocks until I can feel its warmth in my bones.

(Wendell Berry, "An Entrance to the Woods")

Hymn

Will there really be a "Morning"?
Is there such a thing as "Day"?
Could I see it from the mountains
If I were as tall as they?

Has it feet like Water lilies?
Has it feathers like a Bird?
Is it brought from famous countries
Of which I have never heard?

Oh some Scholar! Oh some Sailor!
Oh some Wise Man from the skies!
Please to tell a little Pilgrim
Where the place called "Morning" lies!

(Emily Dickinson)

Closing

Thank you, God, for the promise of the day that you hold before me with the first blush of light. My spirit is fresh and open, having taken time to behold the beauty of the morning and to give thanks for the joy of being alive.

Blessings

Opening

Blessed be all your creation, O God.
Blessed be the fields in harvest,
Blessed be the animals we befriend,
Blessed be the seeds we plant and the food we eat.
Blessed be all the goodness of the world, O God.

Psalm

God, show your faithfulness, bless us,
and make your face smile on us!
For then the earth will acknowledge your ways,
and all the nations will know of your power to save.

. . . .

The soil has given its harvest;
God, our God, has blessed us.
May God continue to bless us;
and let God be feared to the very ends of the earth.

(Psalm 67)

Reading

Your enjoyment of the world is never right till
every morning you awake in heaven, see yourself
in [God's] palace, and look upon the skies and the

earth and the air as celestial joys, having such a reverend esteem of all as if you were among the angels.

(Thomas Traherne)

Hymn

"Blessed be you, harsh matter, barren soil, stubborn rock: you who yield only to violence, you who force us to work if we would eat. . . .

"Blessed be you, mighty matter, irresistible march of evolution, reality ever new-born; you who, by constantly shattering our mental categories, force us to go ever further and further in our pursuit of the truth.

"Blessed be you, universal matter, immeasurable time, boundless ether, . . . you who by overflowing and dissolving our narrow standards or measurement reveal to us the dimensions of God. . . .

". . . I bless you, matter, and you I acclaim: not as the pontiffs of science or the moralizing preachers depict you, debased, disfigured—a mass of brute forces and base appetites—but as you reveal yourself to me today, *in your totality and your true nature.*"

(Pierre Teilhard de Chardin, Hymn of the Universe)

Closing

I turn to you, O God, realizing that you are the creator of all things. You are the protector and nurturer of the world. Bless us when we break our bond with nature, and help us to see your creative energy at the center of every physical reality. Grant us the ability to embrace the earth with compassion and generosity.

Spring

Opening

O Giver of Life, let me remain open to the birth,
fresh innocence, and fullness of the world and of
my own heart. Release me from the blindness that
prevents me from seeing the renewal of the earth
and the transformation of my inner life.

Psalm

Sing to God with thanksgiving;
sing praise with the harp to our God,
who covers the heavens with clouds,
who provides rain for the earth,
and who makes grass grow on the mountains,
who gives food to the cattle,
and to the young ravens when they call.

(Psalm 147:7–9)

Reading

One attraction in coming to the woods to live was
that I should have leisure and opportunity to see
the spring come in. The ice in the pond at length
begins to be honey-combed, and I can set my heel
in it as I walk. Fogs and rains and warmer suns are
gradually melting the snow; the days have grown
sensibly longer; and I see how I shall get through
the winter without adding to my wood-pile, for
large fires are no longer necessary. I am on alert
for the first signs of spring, to hear the chance note
of some arriving bird, or the striped squirrel's
chirp, for his stores must be now nearly exhausted,

or see the woodchuck venture out of his winter quarters.

(Henry David Thoreau, *Walden*)

Hymn

Nothing is so beautiful as spring—
    When weeds, in wheels, shoot long and lovely
        and lush;
    Thrush's eggs look little low heavens, and thrush
Through the echoing timber does so rinse and wring
The ear, it strikes like lightnings to hear him sing;
    The glassy peartree leaves and blooms, they
        brush
    The descending blue; that blue is all in a rush
With richness; the racing lambs too have fair their
        fling.
What is all this juice and all this joy?
    A strain of the earth's sweet being in the
        beginning
In Eden garden. . . .

(Gerard Manley Hopkins, "Spring")

Closing

O God, give us the wisdom to bring forth all that lies fallow in the land and in our heart and to respect the earth and the gift of our life.

Seedtime

Opening

God of hope, I watch the buried seeds draw upward through the earth's crust, answering a promise of new life. Burgeoning plants catch my attention, and my spirit flowers.

Psalm

You have cared for the land and watered it;
greatly you have enriched it.
God's streams are filled;
you have provided the grain.
Thus have you prepared the land:
drenching its furrows,
breaking up its clods,
softening it with showers,
blessing its yield.
You have crowned the year with your bounty
and with abundant harvest.
The fallow meadows overflow,
and gladness clothes the hills.
The fields are arrayed with flocks,
and the valleys blanketed with grain.
They shout and sing for joy.

(Psalm 65:9–13)

Reading

Yesterday for the first time this spring I went out and did a little raking—raking leaves off a place where I have planted a row of crocuses this year. Then I took some salt hay off the upper border, and luckily I did so, for the white heather is in flower. I brought in a few branches of forsythia in bud.

Today is a gentle gray day, with rain expected, but I hope to manage an hour's work outdoors before it comes, at least fertilize the azaleas. . . . I feel like sowing-mix in which some random seeds may have been planted, but none have "taken."

(May Sarton, *The House by the Sea*)

Hymn

Lord, in this splendid season
When all the things that grow extend their arms
  and show the world Your love,

Shall the free wills of men alone
Bide in their January ice
And keep the stubborn winter of their fruitlessness?

Why are we all afraid of love?
Why should we, who are far greater than the grain
Fear to fall in the ground and die?

(Thomas Merton,
"The Transformation: For the Sacred Heart")

Closing

Awaken the seeds planted in the secret depths of my heart, living God. Help me to rise like shoots from the seeds, fulfilling the rhythm of the earth and answering the promise of new life.

Wildflowers

Opening

Enthusiasm for wildflowers is contagious, O God. The miraculous existence of a forest violet is a wonder. Purest color springs from its translucent petals. Help me become mindful of all things that blossom, making the world a garden.

Psalm

"Think how the flowers grow; they never have to spin or weave; yet, I assure you, not even Solomon in all his royal robes was clothed like one of them."

(Luke 12:27)

Reading

The inner surface of the Adonis-blood anemone is as fine as velvet, and yet there is no suggestion of pile, not as much as on a velvet rose. And from this inner smoothness issues the red colour, perfectly pure and unknown of earth, no earthiness, and yet solid, not transparent. How a colour manages to be perfectly strong and impervious, yet of a purity that suggests condensed light, yet not luminous, at least, not transparent, is a problem. The poppy in her radiance is translucent, and the tulip in her utter redness has a touch of opaque earth. But the Adonis-blood anemone is neither translucent nor opaque. It is just pure condensed red, of a velvetiness without velvet, and a scarlet without glow.

(D. H. Lawrence, *Flowery Tuscany*)

Hymn

White with daisies and red with sorrel
   And empty, empty under the sky!—
Life is a quest and love a quarrel—
   Here is a place for me to lie.

Daisies spring from damnèd seeds,
   And this red fire that here I see
Is a worthless crop of crimson weeds,
   Cursed by farmers thriftily.

But here, unhated for an hour,
   The sorrel runs in ragged flame,
The daisy stands, a bastard flower,
   Like flowers that bear an honest name.

And here a while, where no wind brings
   The baying of a pack athirst,
May sleep the sleep of blessèd things,
   The blood too bright, the brow accurst.
                    (Edna St. Vincent Millay, "Weeds")

Closing

Thank you, O Creator, for the radiance of wildflowers: snapdragons, violets, columbine, wood
lily, iris, painted trillium, jack-in-the-pulpit. Their
petals, brilliant, almost translucent in the sunlight,
wave in the breeze like small faces. I see their frag-
ile beauty, forget myself, but remember you.

Gardens

Opening

O gracious God, I am filled with the delight of gardens—a circus of scents and brilliant colors, a home for fertility, sunshine, and song. Gardens bring me home to the earth.

Psalm

Awake, north wind,
come, wind of the south!
Breathe over my garden,
to spread its sweet smell around.
Let my love come into his garden,
let him taste its most exquisite fruits.

(Song of Songs 4:16)

Reading

Odd as I am sure it will appear to some, I can think of no better form of personal involvement in the cure of the environment than that of gardening. A person who is growing a garden, if he is growing it organically, is improving a piece of the world. He is producing something to eat, which makes him somewhat independent of the grocery business, but he is also enlarging, for himself, the meaning of food and the pleasure of eating.

(Wendell Berry, *A Continuous Harmony*)

Hymn

Who would have thought my shrivelled heart
Could have recovered greenness? It was gone
   Quite under ground; as flowers depart
To see their mother-root, when they have blown;
      Where they together
      All the hard weather,
   Dead to the world, keep house unknown.

. . . .

These are thy wonders, Lord of love,
To make us see we are but flowers that glide:
   Which when we once can find and prove,
Thou hast a garden for us, where to bide.
          (George Herbert, "The Flower")

Closing

O God, gardens help us discover an inner place, a
secret garden of silent enjoyment. Thank you for
drawing me into the garden of your creative love.

In Wonder

Opening

Creator of all life, I pray for wonder toward my life and the natural world. I am aware of the mental categories and cultural clichés that allow me to take life for granted and forget the amazing reality around me. Grant me a rebirth of wonder, so that I remember you "who measured the water of the sea in the hollow of your hand and calculated the dimensions of the heavens" (adapted from Isaiah 40:12).

Psalm

"Where were you when I laid the earth's
   foundations?
   Tell me, since you are so well-informed!
Who decided its dimensions, do you know?
   Or who stretched the measuring line across it?
What supports its pillars at their bases?
   Who laid its cornerstone
to the joyful concert of the morning stars
   and unanimous acclaim of the [children] of God?"
(Job 38:4–7)

Reading

A child's world is fresh and new and beautiful, full of wonder and excitement. It is our misfortune that for most of us that clear-eyed vision, that true instinct for what is beautiful and awe-inspiring, is dimmed and even lost before we reach adulthood. If I had influence with the good fairy who is supposed to preside over the christening of all children I should ask that her gift to each child in the world be a sense of wonder so indestructible that it would last throughout life, as an unfailing antidote against the boredom and disenchantments of later years, the sterile preoccupation with things that are artificial, the alienation from the sources of our strength.

(Rachel Carson, *The Sense of Wonder*)

Hymn

How like an angel came I down!
   How bright are all things here!
When first among His works I did appear
   O how their glory did me crown!
The world resembled His eternity,
   In which my soul did walk;
And everything that I did see
   Did with me talk.

The skies in their magnificence,
   The lively, lovely air;
O how divine, how soft, how sweet, how fair!
   The stars did entertain my sense,
And all the works of God so bright and pure,
   So rich and great did seem,
As if they ever must endure
   In my esteem.

(Thomas Traherne, "Wonder")

Closing

O God, nature's mystery confronts me at all times and everywhere. Reasoning fails, and wonder reigns. Open my life to childlike wonder, so that I can continue to travel the way of faith.

Water

Opening

O Creator, cool water on my lips refreshes my spirit
and captures my imagination. Help me remain
conscious of this sweet liquid that flows from the
mountains, springs, and out of the earth's depths
to give us birth and life.

Psalm

"Whoever drinks this water
will get thirsty again;
but those who drink the water I shall give
will never be thirsty again;
the water that I shall give
will turn into a spring inside them, welling up to
   eternal life."

(Adapted from John 4:13–14)

Reading

"I am thirsty for this water," said the little prince.
"Give me some of it to drink. . . ."

And I understood what he had been looking for.

I raised the bucket to his lips. He drank, his eyes
closed. It was as sweet as some special festival
treat. This water was indeed a different thing from
ordinary nourishment. Its sweetness was born of
the walk under the stars, the song of the pulley, the
effort of my arms. It was good for the heart, like a
present.

(Antoine de Saint Exupéry, *The Little Prince*)

Hymn

What a girl called "the dailiness of life"
(Adding an errand to your errand. Saying,
"Since you're up . . ." Making you a means to
A means to a means to) is well water
Pumped from an old well at the bottom of the
    world.
The pump you pump the water from is rusty
And hard to move and absurd, a squirrel-wheel
A sick squirrel turns slowly, through the sunny
Inexorable hours. And yet sometimes
The wheel turns of its own weight, the rusty
Pump pumps over your sweating face the clear
Water, cold, so cold! you cup your hands
And gulp from them the dailiness of life.

(Randall Jarrell, "Well Water")

Closing

Eternal God, thank you for the refreshment of
water. It offers hope and rebirth. Water gathers
force within; it is my way and my life. The sound
of flowing water reminds me to yield and remain
open to the healing presence of your grace.

Fire

Opening

When sitting by the fireside and contemplating the dancing flames, loving God, I am entranced by the sudden changes, the dynamic movement, and the intoxicating light. Teach me how to listen to the voice at the heart of the flame and to learn the language of light: "Come, let us walk in Yahweh's light" (Isaiah 2:5).

Psalm

Yahweh preceded them,
by day in a pillar of cloud to show them the way,
and by night in a pillar of fire to give them light,
so that they could march by day and by night.
The pillar of cloud never left its place ahead of the
    people during the day,
nor the pillar of fire during the night.

(Exodus 13:21–22)

Reading

The fire confined to the fireplace was no doubt for [humans] the first object of reverie, the symbol of repose, the invitation to repose. . . . To be deprived of a reverie before a burning fire is to lose the first use and the truly human use of fire. To be sure, a fire warms us and gives us comfort. But one only becomes fully aware of this comforting sensation after quite a long period of contemplation of the flames; one only receives comfort from the fire when one leans his elbows on his knees and holds his head in his hands. This attitude comes from the distant past. The child by the fire assumes it naturally. Not for nothing is it the attitude of the Thinker. It leads to a very special kind of attention which has nothing in common with the attention involved in watching or observing.

(Gaston Bachelard, *The Psychoanalysis of Fire*)

Hymn

The deer were bounding like blown leaves
Under the smoke in front of the roaring waves of
    the brush-fire;
I thought of the smaller lives that were caught.
Beauty is not always lovely; the fire was beautiful,
    the terror
Of the deer was beautiful; and when I returned
Down the black slopes after the fire had gone by,
    an eagle
Was perched on the jag of a burnt pine,
Insolent and gorged, cloaked in the folded storms
    of his shoulders.
He had come from far off for the good hunting
With fire for his beater to drive the game; the sky
    was merciless
Blue, and the hills merciless black,
The sombre-feathered great bird sleepily merciless
    between them.
I thought, painfully, but the whole mind,
The destruction that brings an eagle from heaven
    is better than mercy.

(Robinson Jeffers, "Fire on the Hills")

Closing

God of fire,
let me accept the white and blue flames
that offer me the opportunity to change,
and draw my life to death and renewal.

Wind

Opening

This blast of wind remains invisible, O God,
though I know it by its effects. The wind makes tall
grass sway on a summer day, whips a lake into a
frenzy, and causes an autumn leaf to jump and
swirl. The wind also has an enormous freedom,
going its own way and playing where it pleases.
Wind of God, blow into my soul.

Psalm

"The wind blows where it pleases;
you can hear its sound,
but you cannot tell where it comes from or where it
   is going.
So it is with everyone who is born of the Spirit."

(John 3:8)

Reading

You do not know the power of the wind until you
get into some high upland where it is always blowing. Then you see, in the sparse grass, the shining
reflection of stones on which no lichen can secure
a foothold. The rocks have lain there for ages while
the wind has passed over them until, like pebbles
in a stream, they have been polished by the mere

passage of an unseen thing—the air. Lift them up and turn them over and the underside has the rough, crusty appearance of the original stone. It is a testimony to time and the passage of invisible powers.

(Loren Eiseley)

Hymn

When great Nature sighs, we hear the winds
Which, noiseless in themselves,
Awaken voices from other beings,
Blowing on them.
From every opening
Loud voices sound. Have you not heard
This rush of tones?
(Thomas Merton, "The Breath of Nature")

Closing

Spirit of God, you are the wind that sweeps through my life. I pray for the strength to accept and respond to your influence. I feel the fresh breeze against my face and remember that my life is changing even now, constantly being transformed in time.

Light

Opening

O God, you who are light, open my eyes so I can
see your divine light that penetrates the world,
revealing infinite possibilities. Make my eyes gentle and my heart expansive, so that I can know the
radiance, the shimmering tide of light, that offers
timelessness and transcendent love.

Psalm

Bless Yahweh, O my soul.
How great you are, Yahweh, my God!
You are clothed in majesty and splendor,
wrapped in a robe of light!

(Psalm 104:1–2)

Reading

The aurora borealis, pale gossamer curtains of
light that seem to undulate across the arctic skies,
are transfixing in part because of their diffidence.
"It is impossible to witness such a beautiful phe-
nomenon without a sense of awe," wrote Robert
Scott, the British Antarctic explorer, "and yet this
sentiment is not inspired by its brilliancy but
rather by its delicacy in light and colour, its trans-
parency, and above all by its tremulous evanes-
cence of form. There is no glittering splendour to
dazzle the eye, as has been too often described;
rather the appeal is to the imagination by the
suggestion of something wholly spiritual."

(Barry Lopez, *Arctic Dreams*)

Hymn

I saw Eternity the other night
Like a great *Ring* of pure and endless light,
   All calm, as it was bright,
And round beneath it, Time in hours, days, years
     Driven by the spheres
Like a vast shadow moved, in which the world
   And all her train were hurled.

             (Henry Vaughan, "The World")

Closing

Glorious God, let me bathe in light, the penetrating light that suffuses the body and extends outward into the world. Thank you for the radiance that illuminates all reality and floods the vulnerable heart.

Stones

Opening

O God, you bless us with this rich earth, with the soil, flora, and rock that offer us security and life. With all the earth, from the smallest pebble to the greatest mountain, I praise you, the rock of my salvation.

Psalm

"Now I shall lay a stone in Zion,
a granite stone, a precious corner-stone,
a firm foundation-stone:
no one who relies on this will stumble.
And I will make fair judgement the measure,
and uprightness the plumb-line."

(Isaiah 28:16–17)

Reading

Rock shows [us] something that transcends the precariousness of [our] humanity: an absolute mode of being. Its strength, its motionlessness, its size and its strange outlines are none of them human; they indicate the presence of something that fascinates, terrifies, attracts and threatens, all at once. In its grandeur, its hardness, its shape and its colour, [we] are faced with a reality and a force that belong to some world other than the profane world of which [we are ourselves] a part.

(Mircea Eliade, *Patterns in Comparative Religion*)

Hymn

How happy is the little Stone
That rambles in the Road alone,
And doesn't care about Careers
And Exigencies never fears—
Whose Coat of elemental Brown
A passing Universe put on,
And independent as the Sun
Associates or glows alone,
Fulfilling absolute Decree
In casual simplicity—

(Emily Dickinson)

Closing

O God, rock of your people, let me learn from
stones and rocks, boulders and pebbles, a wisdom
that cannot be found elsewhere. May I learn of my
uniqueness and relish simplicity. Let me find revelation in this seemingly insignificant object of
nature.

The Drama of Trees

Opening

O God, among the trees I can listen to the wind,
the birds, and the streams. Open my heart to the
secret power of trees, their relationship to earth
and sky, their silent witness to you.

Psalm

The just flourish like a palm tree,
they grow tall as a cedar of Lebanon.
Planted as they are in the house of the Creator,
they flourish in the courts of our God,
bearing fruit in old age like trees full of sap—
vigorous, wide-spreading—
eager to declare that Yahweh is just,
my Rock, in whom there is no wrong.

(Psalm 92:12–15)

Reading

I want to think about trees. Trees have a curious
relationship to the subject of the present moment.
There are many created things in the universe that
outlive us, that outlive the sun, even, but I can't
think about them. I live with trees. There are creatures under our feet, creatures that live over our
heads, but trees live quite convincingly in the
same filament of air we inhabit, and, in addition,
they extend impressively in both directions, up
and down, shearing rock and fanning air, doing
their real business just out of reach. A blind man's
idea of hugeness is a tree. They have their sturdy

bodies and special skills; they garner fresh water;
they abide.

(Annie Dillard, *Pilgrim at Tinker Creek*)

Hymn

"'From the top of the tall cedar tree,
from the highest branch I shall take a shoot
and plant it myself on a high and lofty mountain.
I shall plant it on the highest mountain in Israel.
It will put out branches and bear fruit
and grow into a noble cedar tree.
Every kind of bird will live beneath it,
every kind of winged creature will rest in the shade
    of its branches.
And all the trees of the countryside will know
    that I, Yahweh, am the one
who lays the tall tree low and raises the low tree
    high,
who makes the green tree wither and makes the
    withered
    bear fruit.'"

(Ezekiel 17:22–24)

Closing

O God, thank you for the beauty and wonder of
trees, the shelter and life they provide. May my
faith grow like an oak, strong and enduring; my
love like a pine forest, silent, deep, secretly dependent on you.

The Freedom of Birds

Opening

My God, how beautiful is the lingering flight of a
bird! "'Oh, had I the wings of a dove! Then I would
fly away and be at rest'" (Psalm 55:6).

Psalm

Where could I go to escape your spirit?
Where could I flee from your presence?
If I climb to the heavens, you are there;
there, too, if I sink to Sheol.
If I flew to the point of sunrise—
or far across the sea—
your hand would still be guiding me,
your right hand holding me.

(Psalm 139:7–10)

Reading

Among the many things he spoke to them were
these words that he added: "My brothers, birds,
you should praise your Creator very much and
always love him; he gave you feathers to clothe
you, wings so that you can fly, and whatever else
was necessary for you. God made you noble
among his creatures, and he gave you a home in
the purity of the air; though you neither sow nor

reap, he nevertheless protects and governs you without any solicitude on your part."

(Thomas of Celano, *St. Francis of Assisi*)

Hymn

A Bird came down the Walk—
He did not know I saw—
He bit an Angleworm in halves
And ate the fellow, raw,

And then he drank a Dew
From a convenient Grass—
And then hopped sidewise to the Wall
To let a Beetle pass—

He glanced with rapid eyes
That hurried all around—
They looked like frightened Beads, I thought—
He stirred his Velvet Head

Like one in danger, Cautious,
I offered him a Crumb
And he unrolled his feathers
And rowed him softer home—

Than Oars divide the Ocean,
Too silver for a seam—
Or Butterflies, off Banks of Noon
Leap, plashless as they swim.

(Emily Dickinson)

Closing

My soul sometimes flies like a bird, O God, and I understand what it means to be free in the wind and to eagerly return home to you. May I continue to fly with your wind beneath my wings.

Blessings from the Animals

Opening

My God, let me always see the harmony and interdependence between my life and the lives of all
creatures. I want to love and value the animals
you created, and I want to learn to appreciate
them in their own right, not just for my purposes.
Animals are teachers, and I want to learn.

Psalm

"You have only to ask the cattle, for them to
   instruct you,
 and the birds of the sky, for them to inform you.
The creeping things of earth will give you lessons,
 and the fish of the sea provide you an
   explanation:
there is not one such creature but will know
 that the hand of God has arranged things like
  this!
In [God's] hand is the soul of every living thing
 and the breath of every human being!"
                                            (Job 12:7–10)

Reading

He embraced all things with a rapture of unheard
of devotion, speaking to them of the Lord and
admonishing them to praise him. . . .
  He removed from the road little worms, lest they
be crushed under foot; and he ordered that honey
and the best wines be set out for the bees, lest they
perish from want in the cold of winter. He called

all animals by the name *brother,* though among all the kinds of animals he preferred the gentle. . . .

All creatures, therefore, tried to give their love in return to the saint and to reply by their own gratitude according as he deserved.

(Thomas of Celano, *St. Francis of Assisi*)

Hymn

All he owns is
His body and a few nuts.
He is 300 times as alive as you.
Disney silhouette on a branch,
Headlong creeping, tail afloat, then up, up,
And he sits,
Intensively busy, frisking
Tail, plump tum and small
Able paws. Watch, it's run, ripple, stop,
Stop, run and ripple,
A thousand times a day.
Tired never. Idle never. But always
Squirrel-alert in a close fitting
Comfortable allover fur suit.
All the shut dictionaries reading RODENT
Can't tamp down that
Tail.

(Genevieve Taggard, "Squirrel Near Library")

Closing

Creator God, bless you for all the animals, dainty and ponderous, fierce and peaceable, gaudy and plain. May I never forget my bonds to the animal world, and may I love my "sisters" and "brothers."

Wilderness Sojourn

Opening

O God of love, a wilderness is a place of power and
revelation, a place where you will awaken me to
the energy of your love:

> I am going to seduce her
> and lead her into the desert
> and speak to her heart.

(Hosea 2:16)

Instead of avoiding the lonely, wild places, may I
embrace them in your creation and in myself.
Speak to my heart, God of the wilderness.

Psalm

The people that walked in darkness have seen a
    great light;
on the inhabitants of a country in shadow dark as
    death
  light has blazed forth.
You have enlarged the nation, you have increased
    its joy.

(Isaiah 9:1–2)

Reading

Those of us who have spent time in the wilderness
are aware of the fact that there is something more
to wilderness than we ourselves can express. This is
rooted perhaps in the effect that wilderness has on
human beings who have become estranged from
nature, who live in industrialised environments
and are therefore estranged in a sense from their
natural selves. Wilderness has a profound impact
on them, as well as on those of us more familiar
with it.

. . . Wilderness is an instrument for enabling
us to recover our lost capacity for religious experience.

(Laurens van der Post,
"Wilderness—A Way of Truth")

Hymn

What would the world be, once bereft
Of wet and of wildness? Let them be left,
O let them be left, wildness and wet;
Long live the weeds and the wilderness yet.
(Gerard Manley Hopkins, "Inversnaid")

Closing

Thank you, God, for wilderness as a refuge and
blessing where I can wait alone, pouring out my
heart to you. O God, let wilderness "be left."

Paths

Opening

God, my companion, teach me to follow the path
you set before me, allowing it to lead me to a new
frontier. May I celebrate its rough places and its
smooth places. As I cross over hills, through
streams, and by lost fields and ponds, I am travel-
ing always toward you and with you.

Psalm

Make me know your ways, Yahweh;
teach me your paths.
Lead me in your truth and teach me,
for you are the God of my salvation;
for you I wait all the day long.
Be mindful of your mercy, Yahweh,
and of your steadfast love, for they have been from
of old.

. . . .

All the paths of Yahweh are steadfast love and
faithfulness
for those who keep God's covenant and decrees.

(Psalm 25:4–10)

Reading

Now I yearn for one of those old, meandering, dry,
uninhabited roads, which lead away from towns,
. . . where you may forget in what country you
are travelling; . . . along which you may travel
like a pilgrim, going nowhither; where travellers
are not too often to be met; where my spirit is free;

where the walls and fences are not cared for; where your head is more in heaven than your feet are on earth. . . .

(Henry David Thoreau)

Hymn

Afoot and light-hearted I take to the open road,
Healthy, free, the world before me,
The long brown path before me leading wherever I choose.

Henceforth I ask not good-fortune, I myself am good-fortune,
Henceforth I whimper no more, postpone no more, need nothing,
Done with indoor complaints, libraries, querulous criticisms,
Strong and content I travel the open road.

(Walt Whitman, "Song of the Open Road")

Closing

O God, I know that the heart is the truest compass. Grant me the wisdom to trust the path itself more than my own interests, and the strength to follow wherever your will leads me. All of life, each path, is an open road if you are with me.

Solitude

Opening

Loving God, give me the strength to remain alone
in this landscape and to allow nature's energy to
stretch my soul, ply it loose from anxiety, boredom, and worry. I breathe deeply and rhythmical-
ly, allowing myself to feel the nearness of the
earth, its thickness and mystery. I look overhead
and watch the billowing clouds travel quietly
through the blue expanse. What feelings drift
through me now!

Psalm

Yahweh, you are my shepherd;
I shall not want.
In verdant pastures you give me repose.
Beside restful waters you lead me;
you refresh my soul.
You guide me in right paths
for your name's sake.

(Psalm 23:1–3)

Reading

To deliver oneself up, to hand oneself over, entrust
oneself completely to the silence of a wide landscape of woods and hills, or sea, or desert; to sit
still while the sun comes up over that land and fills
its silences with light. To pray and work in the
morning and to labor and rest in the afternoon,
and to sit still again in meditation in the evening
when night falls upon that land and when the

silence fills itself with darkness and with stars. This is a true and special vocation.

(Thomas Merton, Thoughts in Solitude)

Hymn

I will arise and go now, and go to Innisfree,
And a small cabin build there, of clay and wattles
    made:
Nine bean-rows will I have there, a hive for the
    honeybee,
And live alone in the bee-loud glade.

And I shall have some peace there, for peace
    comes dropping slow,
Dropping from the veils of the morning to where
    the cricket sings;
There midnight's all a glimmer, and noon a purple
    glow,
And evening full of the linnet's wings.

I will arise and go now, for always night and day
I hear lake water lapping with low sounds by the
    shore;
While I stand on the roadway, or on the
    pavements grey,
I hear it in the deep heart's core.

(William Butler Yeats, "The Lake Isle of Innisfree")

Closing

O God, I am vulnerable to you in the silence of nature, less self-sufficient and more conscious of your presence filling the earth and sky, and flowing within me. Here in the open air, I thank you for the urgency and clarity that fills my heart. I embrace this gift of solitude.

Sacred Places

Opening

O God, you lead me to this sacred ground where I can be alone and calm my noisy heart. You have drawn me to this place so that your silence can fill my being. Allow me to remain open to your revelation. Remind me occasionally that all of your earth is holy ground.

Psalm

The world and all that is in it belong to Yahweh,
the earth and all who live on it.
Yahweh built it on the deep waters,
laid its foundations in the oceans' depths.
Who has the right to climb Yahweh's mountain?
Or stand in this holy place?
Those who are pure in act and in thought,
who do not worship idols
or make false promises.

(Psalm 24:1–4)

Reading

The sun was almost setting when we came to the hill, and the old man helped me make the place where I was to stand. We went to the highest point of the hill and made the ground there sacred by spreading sage upon it. . . .

Few Tails now told me what I was to do so that the spirits would hear me and make clear my next duty. I was to stand in the middle, crying and praying for understanding. Then I was to advance from the center to the quarter of the west and mourn there awhile. Then I was to back up to the center, and from there approach the quarter of the north, wailing and praying there, and so on all around the circle. This I had to do all night long.

(*Black Elk Speaks*)

Hymn

Jacob took a stone for a pillow,
put it under his head, and went to sleep.
As he dreamed, God told him,
"Know that I am here with you
in this place
and wherever you will go.
I will not leave you."
Jacob awoke from his sleep and said,
"How amazing this place is!
This is nothing less than the house of God;
this is the gate of heaven!"
Rising early in the morning,
Jacob took the stone he had used for his pillow,
and set it up as a monument.

(Adapted from Genesis 28:15–18)

Closing

Loving God, following my heart's longing, I discover you anew in this place. Thank you for the revelation of this holy ground. How wonderful is this place.

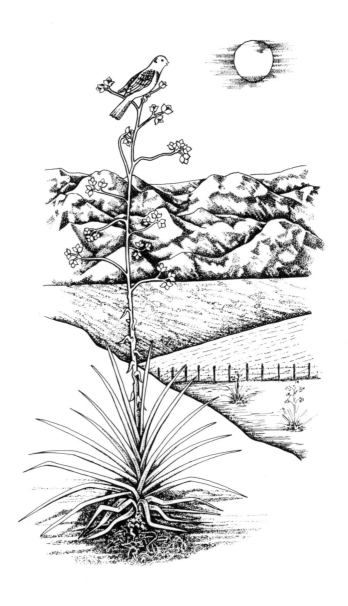

Mountains

Opening

God, my eye is on the path as I climb, but I also notice the awesome beauty rising before me. Looking at the summit, I think of the power of the Holy and the reality of my highest goal.

Psalm

For you, O God, are my stronghold.
Why do you keep me so far away?
Why must I go about in mourning,
oppressed by the enemy?
Send forth your light and your truth—
they shall guide me;
let them bring me to your holy mountain,
to your dwelling place.

(Psalm 43:2–3)

Reading

Mountains are, to the rest of the body of the earth, what violent muscular action is to the body. . . . The muscles and tendons of its anatomy are, in the mountain, brought out with fierce and convulsive energy, full of expression, passion, and strength; the plains and the lower hills are the repose and the effortless motion of the frame, when its muscles lie dormant and concealed beneath the lines of its beauty, yet ruling those lines in their every undulation. This, then, is the first grand principle of the truth of the earth.

(John Ruskin, *Modern Painters*)

Hymn

That mountain there,
That white-shell mountain,
Toward the east it standeth,
O sacred mountain,
Whence the day springs.
O white-shell mountain,
Guard thou our day!

Yonder, afar,
That dark blue mountain,
Toward the north standing
That sacred mountain,
Whence the storm cometh,
O dark blue mountain,
Spare not our storm!

That mountain there,
That turquoise-colored mountain,
Toward the west it standeth,
The path of life unending
And beyond it,
O turquoise mountain,
Guide thou our way!

Yonder, afar,
Rose-yellow mountain,
Sacred southern mountain,
Yonder afar, in beauty walking,
The way of joy unending;
Rose-yellow mountain,
Keep thou our home!

(Woman's Dance at Tesuque Pueblo,
"Pilgrimage Song")

Closing

God, my dreams begin and end with mountains. Mountains do not allow my psyche any rest. Their hugeness and wildness remind me of your power and my vulnerability. Seeing these worlds of rock and ice, I cast myself on your eternal mercy, knowing that your love is larger than any summit.

At the Shore

Opening

O God, I listen for your revelation in the crashing
waves as they merge with the shore, blanket large
rocks, and pull at loose driftwood. Open my heart
to the compelling voice of the sea.

Psalm

The seas have lifted up, O Yahweh,
the seas have lifted up their voice;
the seas have lifted up their pounding waves.
More powerful than the thunder of the great waters,
mightier than the breakers of the sea—
Yahweh is powerful on high.

(Psalm 93:3–4)

Reading

The edge of the sea is a strange and beautiful
place. All through the long history of Earth it has
been an area of unrest where waves have broken
heavily against the land, where tides have pressed
forward over the continents, receded, and then
returned. For no two successive days is the shore
line precisely the same. . . .
  The shore is an ancient world, for as long as
there has been an earth and sea there has been
this place of the meeting of land and water. Yet it
is a world that keeps alive the sense of continuing
creation and of the relentless drive of life. Each
time that I enter it, I gain some new awareness of
its beauty and its deeper meanings, sensing that

intricate fabric of life by which one creature is
linked with another, and each with its surroundings.

(Rachel Carson, The Edge of the Sea)

Hymn

On the beach at night alone,
As the old mother sways her to and fro singing her
      husky song,
As I watch the bright stars shining, I think a
      thought of the clef of the universes and of the
      future.
A vast similitude interlocks all,
All spheres, grown, ungrown, small, large, suns,
      moons, planets,
. . . .
All distances of time, all inanimate forms,
All souls, all living bodies though they be ever so
      different,
   or in different worlds,
. . . .
All identities that have existed or may exist on this
      globe, or any globe
All lives and deaths, all of the past, present, future,
This vast similitude spans them, and always has
      spann'd,
And shall forever span them and compactly hold
      and enclose them.
  (Walt Whitman, "On the Beach at Night Alone")

Closing

O God, the waves speak to my heart. They rise,
gain momentum, fall, and draw me into deeper
levels of consciousness. Thank you for this place of

rhythm and harmony, a place I can retreat to when my life seems confused and overwhelming. May I be rocked back and forth and soothed as a child in your ever-loving arms.

Reclaiming a Rich Land

Opening

Gracious God, you promised your people a fertile
land, a land of promise, a land that would flourish
under your attentive eye. May I learn to respect
and appreciate the land that you have given us
and see it as a sign of your loving attention.

Psalm

"But Yahweh your God
is bringing you into a fine country,
a land of streams and springs,
of waters that well up from the deep in valleys and
    hills,
a land of wheat and barley,
of vines, of figs, of pomegranates,
a land of olives, of oil, of honey,
a land where you will eat bread without stint,
where you will want nothing."

(Deuteronomy 8:7–9)

Reading

In relation to the earth, we have been autistic for
centuries. Only now have we begun to listen with
some attention and with a willingness to respond

to the earth's demands that we cease our industrial assault, that we abandon our inner rage against the conditions of our earthly existence, that we renew our human participation in the grand liturgy of the universe.

(Thomas Berry, *The Dream of the Earth*)

Hymn

The world is charged with the grandeur of God.
   It will flame out, like shining from shook foil;
   It gathers to a greatness, like the ooze of oil
Crushed. Why do men then now not reck his rod?
Generations have trod, have trod, have trod;
    And all is seared with trade; bleared, smeared
      with toil;
    And wears man's smudge and shares man's
      smell: the soil
Is bare now, nor can foot feel, being shod.
And for all this, nature is never spent;
    There lives the dearest freshness deep down
      things. . . .

(Gerard Manley Hopkins, "God's Grandeur")

Closing

Gracious God, you offer us the seasons, the planting and harvesting of crops, as well as participation in the earth's cycle. This fertile land is your divine blessing. May we listen to the earth's demands and love the earth as we love ourselves. Thank you.

New Heaven, New Earth

Opening

Eternal God, maker of heaven and earth, you draw
all creation toward you, according to your plan
and purpose. Help me to uncover a hopeful vision
for the whole earth, a time when all things will be
made new.

Psalm

Yahweh, how many are the works you have created,
arranging everything in wisdom!

. . . .

All creatures depend on you
to give them food in due season.
You give the food they eat;
with generous hand, you fill them with good things.
If you turn your face away—they suffer;
if you stop their breath—they die and return to dust.
When you give your spirit, they are created.
You keep renewing the world.
Glory forever to you, Yahweh!

(Psalm 104:24–31)

Reading

Then I was standing on the highest mountain of
them all, and round about beneath me was the
whole hoop of the world. And while I stood there I
saw more than I can tell and I understood more
than I saw; for I was seeing in a sacred manner the
shapes of all things in the spirit, and the shape of
all shapes as they must live together like one be-

ing. And I saw that the sacred hoop of my people was one of many hoops that made one circle, wide as daylight and as starlight, and in the center grew one mighty flowering tree to shelter all the children of one mother and one father. And I saw that it was holy.

(Black Elk Speaks)

Hymn

The wolf will live with the lamb,
the panther lie down with the kid,
calf, lion and fat-stock beast together,
with a little [child] to lead them.
The cow and the bear will graze,
their young will lie down together.
The lion will eat hay like the ox.
The infant will play over the den of the adder;
the baby will put [its] hand into the viper's lair.
No hurt, no harm will be done
on all my holy mountain,
for the country will be full of knowledge of Yahweh
as the waters cover the sea.

(Isaiah 11:6–9)

Closing

O God, I realize that the transformation of heaven and earth will not happen only at the end of time, but that the earth is constantly being renewed and all things visible and invisible are being drawn to you for consummation in Christ. Renew your world, gracious God, and renew my spirit. Alleluia!

Earth Community

Opening

Creator of all life, help me to understand that I am
not self-sufficient but live in a world created by
you, a world of animals, mountains, seas, and
prairies, a world of participants in your creative
love. Help me to realize that no matter how remote
or indifferent I might feel, I am intimately related
to the entirety of creation.

Psalm

Yahweh, you are good to all
and have compassion on all your works.
All your works give you thanks, O God,
and your faithful ones bless you.
They discourse on the glory of your reign
and speak of your might.

. . . .
The eyes of all look hopefully to you,
and you give them bread in due season.
You open your hand
and satisfy the desire of every living thing.
Yahweh, you are just in all your ways
and loving in all your works.

(Psalm 145:9–17)

Reading

Science is providing some of our most powerful
poetic references and metaphoric expressions.
Scientists suddenly have become aware of the
magic quality of the earth and of the universe
entire.

. . . From the tiniest fragment of matter to the grand sweep of the galactic systems, we have a new clarity through our empirical modes of knowing. We are more intimate with every particle of the universe and with the vast design of the whole. We see it and hear it and commune with it as never before. Not only in its spatial extension, but in its emergent process, we are intimate with the world about us.

(Thomas Berry, *The Dream of the Earth*)

Hymn

The Earth is my Mother,
She will always be near.
The Sun, my Father,
I have nothing to fear.
The Moon is my Sister,
Standing with me at night.
The Stars are my Cousins
Who guide me in flight.
The Great Spirit is my God
Of life and of love.

(Raymond Hamilton, "As Once, So Were We")

Closing

O God, may this communal consciousness with the planet inspire me to find the sacred at the center of the world. I commit myself to protect and tend to the environment, just as I would protect and tend to my sister, brother, mother, and father.

Earthsong

Opening

O Creator, the earth responds to your revelation.
The earth is alive and dynamic, singing praise
to you.

Psalm

All things that God made, bless your God,
give God glory and thunderous ovation.
Night and day, bless your God,
give God glory and thunderous ovation.
You, light and darkness, bless your God,
give God glory and thunderous ovation.
Lightning and rain clouds, bless your God,
give God glory and thunderous ovation.
You, grateful earth, bless your God,
give God glory and thunderous ovation.

(Adapted from Daniel 3:57,71–74)

Reading

The words of the psalms were not just sounds; the
words were images, images of the world, images of
God. The brief verses flashed in and out of the
liturgy of the Catholic mass like bright melodic
intrusions into the long rhetorical portions of the
service. They told me that rivers clapped their
hands and trees shouted for joy, hills leapt like
yearling lambs and heaven sang. Days told stories
and messages blew through the night wind.

(Meinrad Craighead, *The Litany of the Great River*)

Hymn

A song of the rolling earth, and of words according,
Were you thinking that those were the words, those
    upright lines?
        those curves, angles, dots?
No, those are not the words, the substantial words
    are in the
        ground and sea,
They are in the air, they are in you.

. . . .

Air, soil, water, fire—those are words,
I myself am a word with them—my qualities
    interpenetrate with
        theirs—my name is nothing to them,
Though it were told in the three thousand
    languages, what would
        air, soil, water, fire, know of my name?
        (Walt Whitman, "A Song of the Rolling Earth")

Closing

O God, teach me to see the earth not as property, but as a participant in your revelation. Realizing the interdependence between my own life and that of the planet, I discover an earth filled with song. Orchestrated skies, rhythmic landscapes, the music of mountains, skies, seas, and deserts enter into my prayer. Glory and praise to you, Creator of earth's singing.

Sun, Moon, and Stars

Opening

O God, open my heart to the sun, moon, and stars
as they proclaim your glory day after day. They
sing no words: their light is their voice. The sky
resonates with a song that rings in the valleys,
rises from the hills, and merges with rivers and
streams.

Psalm

Praise God from the heavens;
praise God in the heights;
praise God, all you angels;
praise God, all you heavenly hosts.
Praise God, sun and moon;
praise God, all you shining stars.
Praise God, you highest heavens,
and you waters above the heavens.
Let them praise the name of God,
who commanded and they were created.

(Psalm 148:1–5)

Reading

March 12—A fine sunset: the higher sky dead clear
blue bridged by a broad slant causeway rising
from right to left of wisped or grass cloud, the
wisps lying across; the sundown yellow, moist with
light but ending at the top in a foam of delicate
white pearling and spotted with big tufts of cloud
in colour russet between brown and purple but

edged with brassy light. But what I note it all for is this: before I had always taken the sunset and the sun as quite out of gauge with each other, . . . but today I inscaped them together and made the sun the true eye and ace of the whole, as it is.

(Gerard Manley Hopkins)

Hymn

Most High, all-powerful, good Lord,
Yours are the praises, the glory, the honor, and all
blessing.
To You alone, Most High, do they belong,
and no man is worthy to mention Your name.
Praised be You, my Lord, with all your creatures,
especially Sir Brother Sun,
Who is the day and through whom You give us
light.
And he is beautiful and radiant with great splendor;
and bears a likeness of You, Most High One.
Praised be You, my Lord, through Sister Moon and
the stars,
in heaven You formed them clear and precious
and beautiful.

(Francis of Assisi, "The Canticle of Brother Sun")

Closing

Holy God, thank you for the radiance of the sun, moon, and stars. Face to face with the beauty of the sky, I feel your glory, which surpasses all that I have ever known. Thank you for the music of the heavens that fills time and space and echoes in my soul.

Vision of the Cosmos

Opening

O God, I pray for a vision that embraces earth, sky, galaxies, countless constellations, the entire luminous universe in you.

Psalm

Praise God from the heavens;
praise God in the heights;
praise God, all you angels;
praise God, all you heavenly hosts.
Praise God, sun and moon;
praise God, all you shining stars.
Praise God, you highest heavens,
and you waters above the heavens.

(Psalm 148:1–4)

Reading

For me, my God, all joy and all achievement, the very purpose of my being and all my love of life, all depend on this one basic vision of the union between yourself and the universe. Let others, fulfilling a function more august than mine, proclaim your splendours as pure Spirit; as for me, dominated as I am by a vocation which springs from the inmost fibres of my being, I have no desire, I have no ability, to proclaim anything except the innumerable prolongations of your incarnate Being in the world of matter.

(Pierre Teilhard de Chardin, *Hymn of the Universe*)

Hymn

I, the fiery life of divine wisdom,
I ignite the beauty of the plains,
I sparkle the waters,
I burn in the sun, and the moon, and the stars.
With wisdom I order all rightly.

. . . .

I adorn all the earth.
I am the breeze that nurtures all things green.

. . . .

I am the rain coming from the dew
that causes the grasses to laugh with the joy of life.
I call forth tears, the aroma of holy work.
I am the yearning for good.

(Hildegard of Bingen)

Closing

God of hope, may a planetary consciousness help
me to realize my responsibility to meet you at the
center of the world and to work to protect the environment through a new set of values, a new ethic
that moves me beyond self-interest.

Seasons

Opening

Gracious God, seasons pass with such regularity
that I take them for granted. Teach me to experience the seasons fully, to breathe the air deeply, to
taste the food, and to live at the heart of the
changing earth.

Psalm

You made the moon to mark the seasons;
the sun knows the hour of its setting.
You form the shadows, night falls,
and all the forest animals prowl about—
the lions roar for their prey
and seek their food from God.
At sunrise they retire,
to lie down in their lairs.
People go out to work
and to labor until the evening.
Yahweh, how many are the works you have created,
arranging everything in wisdom!

(Psalm 104:19–24)

Reading

You have noticed that everything an Indian does is
in a circle, and that is because the Power of the
World always works in circles, and everything tries
to be round. . . . The sky is round, and I have
heard that the earth is round like a ball, and so
are all the stars. The wind, in its greatest power,
whirls. Birds make their nests in circles, for theirs is

the same religion as ours. The sun comes forth and goes down again in a circle. The moon does the same, and both are round. Even the seasons form a great circle in their changing, and always come back again to where they were. The life of a man is a circle from childhood to childhood, and so it is in everything where power moves.

(Black Elk Speaks)

Hymn

There is a season for everything, a time for every occupation under heaven:

A time for giving birth,
a time for dying;
a time for planting,
a time for uprooting what has been planted.

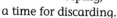

A time for tears,
a time for laughter;
a time for mourning,
a time for dancing.

. . . . . .

A time for searching,
a time for losing;
a time for keeping,
a time for discarding.

(Ecclesiastes 3:1–6)

Closing

My God, I wonder at the cycles in nature and the cycles in my life. Thank you for giving me the time and wisdom to allow these cycles into my heart. I take comfort in them and allow them to refresh my soul.

Storm

Opening

O God, nature erupts. Lightning streaks across the sky, tornados topple houses and trees, hurricanes batter coastlines, earthquakes level entire cities. Are you reminding us how frail we are, how dependent we are on you?

Psalm

Yahweh spoke and raised a gale,
lifting up towering waves.
Tossed to the sky, then plunged to the depths,
they lost their courage in the ordeal,
staggering and reeling like drunkards
with all their skill gone.
Then they cried to Yahweh in their anguish.
Yahweh rescued them from their distress:
reducing the storm to a whisper
the waves grew quiet;
rejoicing at the stillness,
they landed safely at the harbor they desired.

(Psalm 107:25–30)

Reading

We were purged by a magnificent storm all day yesterday. How glorious it was! Fifty-mile gusts of

wind driving the waves in, and almost the highest
tide on record. . . . Judy and I put on boots and
raincoats, and Tamas [the cat] came along, to see
the surf at its height. We could hardly stand
against the wind, our glasses were covered with
salt spray and Tamas' fur was blown back to the
roots. Down at the point we were able to stand for
a few moments with those towering waves roaring
in to right and left, the whole shore white with
foam. It was like an answer to prayer, the outward
storm playing out what might have become an
inward storm had it not absorbed all the tensions,
as it did.

(May Sarton, *The House by the Sea*)

Hymn

When in their ignorance and haste the skies must
   fall
Upon our white-eyed home, and blindly turn
Feeling the four long limits of the wall,

How unsubstantial is our present state
In the clean blowing of those elements
Whose study is our problem and our fate?

(Thomas Merton, "Spring Storm")

Closing

My God, nature sometimes seems like a forsaken,
desolate place, yet in the dark chaos hides a new
and vibrant world. Storms pass through nature
and through my soul. I wait for the clear-washed
blue sky, knowing that you fill nature and me with
life and promise.

Rhythm of Life and Death

Opening

Faithful God, you renew the earth through the universal rhythm of life and death. I must learn to trace all forms of life back to you, the creator and source of all things. May I live in hopeful harmony with your will.

Psalm

All creatures depend on you
to give them food in due season.
You give the food they eat;
with generous hand, you fill them with good things.
If you turn your face away—they suffer;
if you stop their breath—they die and return to dust.
When you give your spirit, they are created.
You keep renewing the world.
Glory forever to you, Yahweh!

(Psalm 104:27–31)

Reading

Everything in the world dies, but we only know about it as a kind of abstraction. If you stand in a meadow, at the edge of a hillside, and look around carefully, almost everything you can catch sight of is in the process of dying, and most things will be dead long before you are. If it were not for the constant renewal and replacement going on before your eyes, the whole place would turn to stone and sand under your feet. . . .

It is a natural marvel. All of the life of the earth dies, all of the time, in the same volume as the new life that dazzles us each morning, each spring. All we see of this is the odd stump, the fly struggling on the porch floor of the summer house in October, the fragment on the highway.

(Lewis Thomas, *The Lives of a Cell*)

Hymn

And if, as autumn deepens and darkens
I feel the pain of falling leaves, and stems that
   break in storms
and trouble and dissolution and distress
and then the softness of deep shadows folding,
   folding
round my soul and spirit, around my lips
so sweet, like a swoon, or more like the drowse of a
   low, sad song
singing darker than the nightingale, on, on to the
   solstice
and the silence of short days, the silence of the
   year, the shadow,
then I shall know that my life is moving still
with the dark earth, and drenched
with the deep oblivion of earth's lapse and renewal.

. . . .

then I must know that still
I am in the hands [of] the unknown God,
he is breaking me down to his own oblivion
to send me forth on a new morning, a new man.

(D. H. Lawrence, "Shadows")

Closing

My life, O God, is like the flower that springs up in the morning and fades by evening. I can see human existence, with all its limitations and finitude, reflected in nature. However, both life and death are grounded in you. Amid this transitoriness, you are the seasonless foundation of my hope.

Winter

Opening

Thank you, God, for blankets of snow that hush all
sound except the babble of the creek. I shuffle
along a path over the reclusive earth, hibernating
at my feet. The naked trees stand at attention in
the brisk wind.

Psalm

Yet, God, my protector from times past,
you bring salvation to the earth.

. . . .

You opened the springs and streams;
you raised dry land out of the waters.
The day and night are yours;
you fashioned the sun and the moon.
You established the bounds of the land;
summer and winter—you make them.

(Psalm 74:12–17)

Reading

Every year the first snow sets me dreaming. By
March it will only bring the grumps, but Novem-
ber snow is revenance, a dreamy restitution of
childhood or even infancy. Tighten the door and
settle a cloth snake against the breeze from the
door's bottom; make sure the storms are firmly
shut; add logs to the stove and widen the draft. Sit
in a chair looking south into blue twilight that
arrives earlier every day—as the sky flakes and
densens, as the first clear flakes float past the

porch's wood to light on dirt of the driveway and on brown frozen grass or dry stalks of the flower border.

(Donald Hall, Seasons at Eagle Pond)

Hymn

The hills sleep
In frozen eiderdowns

I go knee deep in silence
Where the storm smokes and stings
The chattering leaves

You can't rule it
You can't tell it when
To come and go

Sink in the hidden wood
And let the weather
Be what it is

Let seasons go
Far wrong
Let freedom sting
The glad wet eye
Of winter.

(Thomas Merton, "Early Blizzard")

Closing

My God, help me focus my life on the essentials, anchor it in the deepest truth. Pare my heart to the bone, so that I can see the beauty in my life and the beauty in the ice crystals dancing in the afternoon light.

Night Hymn

Opening

O God, the night falling fills my heart and carries it toward an invisible realm. Starlight stirs my eye, and I see a world raining light on my head, on my shoulders, and sifting through my memory, sending me off to unexpected frontiers.

Psalm

Come, bless Yahweh,
all you who serve Yahweh,
ministering in the house of Yahweh,
in the courts of the house of our God!
Lift up your hands toward the sanctuary;
praise Yahweh night after night!
May Yahweh bless you from Zion,
the One who made heaven and earth!

(Psalm 134)

Reading

I was in no tent under leaves, sleepless and glad. There was no moon at all; along the world's coasts the sea tides would be springing strong. The air itself also has lunar tides: I lay still. Could I feel in the air an invisible sweep and surge, and an answering knock in my lungs? Or could I feel the starlight? Every minute on a square mile of this land—on the steers and the orchard, on the quarry, the meadow, and creek—one ten thousandth of an ounce of starlight spatters to earth. What percentage of an ounce did that make on my eyes

and cheeks and arms, tapping and nudging as
particles, pulsing and stroking as waves?

(Annie Dillard, *Pilgrim at Tinker Creek*)

Hymn

O guiding night!
O night more lovely than the dawn!
O night that has united
The lover with his beloved,
Transforming the beloved in her lover.

.   .   .   .

I abandoned and forgot myself
Laying my face on my beloved;
All things ceased; I went out from myself,
Leaving my cares
Forgotten among the lilies.

(John of the Cross)

Closing

God of mystery, in the world of deepening shadow
and starlight I discover solitude again. In the darkness, I find direction toward the secret in my soul.
Thank you for leading me through the threshold of
darkness, where night is transformed into day.

Acknowledgments (*continued*)

The psalms in this book are from *Psalms Anew: In Inclusive Language,* compiled by Nancy Schreck and Maureen Leach (Winona, MN: Saint Mary's Press, 1986). Copyright © 1986 by Saint Mary's Press. All rights reserved.

The scriptural material on pages 26 (opening), 28, 53, and 68 is freely adapted to make it inclusive regarding gender. These adaptations are not to be understood or used as official translations of the Bible.

All other scriptural quotations in this book are from the New Jerusalem Bible. Copyright © 1985 by Darton, Longman and Todd, London; and Doubleday, a division of Bantam, Doubleday, Dell Publishing Group, New York. Reprinted by permission.

The excerpt by Wendell Berry on pages 14–15 is from *Recollected Essays, 1965–1980* (San Francisco: North Point Press, 1981), page 3. Copyright © 1971, 1981 by Wendell Berry. Reprinted by permission of Farrar, Straus and Giroux.

The poems by Emily Dickinson on pages 15, 39, and 43 are from *The Complete Poems of Emily Dickinson,* edited by Thomas H. Johnson (San Francisco: North Point Press, 1960), pages 49–50, 634, and 156, respectively. Copyright © 1960 by Mary L. Hampson.

The excerpts by Thomas Traherne on pages 16–17 and 27 are from *The Selected Writings of Thomas Traherne,* edited by Dick Davis (Manchester, England: Fyfield Books, 1980), pages 75 and 20. Copyright © 1980 by Dick Davis. Used with permission of Carcanet Press.

Society. Used by permission of Viking Penguin, a division of Penguin Books USA.

The excerpt by Donald Hall on pages 82–83 originally appeared in the exhibition catalog *Winter* (Hanover, NH: Hood Museum of Art, Dartmouth College, 1986). Used by permission of Hood Museum of Art.

The excerpt by John of the Cross on page 85 is from *John of the Cross: Selected Writings,* edited by Kieran Kavanaugh (New York: Paulist Press, 1987), pages 55–56. Copyright © 1987 by Kieran Kavanaugh. Used by permission of Paulist Press.